Whispers Between The Lines

Medha Das

BookLeaf
Publishing

India | USA | UK

Made with ❤ on the BookLeaf Publishing Platform
www.bookleafpub.in
www.bookleafpub.com

Dedication

To the one who saw the mess and still called it art.

Preface

This collection was born in the quiet moments between chaos, scribbled in notebooks, typed on my phone at midnight, and pieced together over years of feeling too much or not enough.

These poems explore themes of longing, loss, love, and resilience. They are fragments of experiences, some mine, some imagined, some borrowed from the lives I brushed up against.

I didn't write these poems to be perfect. I wrote them to be real.

Thank you for picking up this book. I hope you find something here that feels like coming home or at the very least, like being understood.

-Medha

Acknowledgements

This book would not exist without the love and patience of the people who stood beside me in the quiet and the chaos.

Thank you to my family, for their unwavering belief in me, even when I doubted myself. To my friends who read early drafts, offered kind words, or simply listened when I needed to speak something out loud, thank you for holding space for me.

Deep gratitude to you, the reader. Whether you stumbled upon this book by chance or sought it out on purpose, thank you for making room in your life for these words. I hope they find you when you need them most.

1. You Are My Tomorrow

It was never me, it was always you.
The things you said, and the things you do.
It was just so mystical, the night we met,
when you lost your way and were distressed.

Buzzing like bees the people around you,
didn't give a second glance to a person so new.
Standing in the heart of the city, the city of joy,
you stood there flustered with not an ounce of joy.

Searching for a way to get back home,
you asked the people around who just looked and
moaned.
Spinning like a ballerina or maybe a damsel in distress,
you walked right up to me making us both hit our
heads.

"Oh, I am so sorry" you said with a trembling voice,
only to take a pause and look into my eyes.
As you stood there in awe,
I snapped you back to life,
"Your eyes" you stuttered "
they are the perfect shade of brown,
I wonder how a pretty girl like you is walking around

with a frown".
It was true, I will not lie.

I had a rough day until this second of life.
Time flew away as we talked for hours,
sharing every inch information of ourselves with each
other.
Day turned to months and months into years,
who knew that day,
that someday you would be,
my today and my tomorrow.

2. Desperation

Yes, it is the silence that echoes in my mind.
Not the fear of attachment but the fear of letting go.
 People call it the art of letting go,
but I wonder is it really though?

Every passing second feels like eternity.
The soul craves your presence my love,
 for the imaginations in my mind only know how to
grow.
The essence of your love, it just never dies.

The aura of your presence surrounds me,
even when you are so far away my love.
 The pain of distance kills me from inside.

Desperation, anticipation with a pinch of love,
is this what they call it the beauty of love?

3. Pain of Separation

Drop by drop.. inch by inch...
It all starts here my love.
How beautiful the summer sun looks as it shines,
and the winter snow as it falls.

How beautiful are the brown autumn
leaves and a new spring Breeze,
o so colourful it was my love,
the day I met you I drowned in love.

The sun shined brighter,
the grass seemed Greener and the air smelled like
lavender.
I couldn't believe that it was real,
it all felt like a dream,
but as everything has a start and an ending this dream
had its ending too.

You said to me "We need to talk"
But little did I know that would be our last talk.
You left me there in full despair, my jaw on the floor.
'Appalled' is that the word when people are going to
have a stroke?
Begging for a second chance I fell on my knees,

but it all felt hopeless when you turned your heart away
from me.

Murdered with a knife stabbed square in the heart,
 I wandered in the empty streets with nothing but a
bleeding heart.
That was the day my love I finally understood,
 love is like a rose,
beautiful from afar but not so pretty up close.
Touch it and you start bleeding yet it is also THE
prettiest rose.

4. Her Life

It's no longer the darkness but now it is light.
Something that seemed so dark is now beautiful to the
sight,
 it brings upon memories some of old,
some lost and some yet to be found.
The stars in the sky,
 they shine so bright,
but the brightest one is you.
 You are the star of my eye.
My dear, the love I hold in my heart is till date
undefined,
 and so will it be for centuries to arrive.
My heart, it craves your soft little touch,
the sound of your laughter and your tears of your cries.
Good and bad, I want it all!
The pain of distance, it kills me inside.
 My heart is bleeding, but not a word in sight.
I am losing time, as seconds go by,
 I will never get back again even if I crib and cry.
Today I stand with my head held high,
knowing that you are now a beautiful person inside and
out.

5. Sweet Lies

Hundreds of thoughts that echo in my mind,
questioning my every decision.
I lay in the lap of a lake full of lies,
just me and my appalled admiration.
I close my eyes and feel the lies that flow through my
body.
Astonished, I endure the delightful endearing sensation.
Easing into consciousness I look towards the lake of
reality.
Suffering from drought it seeks for a crystal droplet.
The sun hangs heavy,
casting a golden sorrow on its barren skin.
Cracks spread like whispers of forgotten truths,
aching for the rain.
Yet the clouds mock the thirst with their silent presence,
Suspended secrets, unwept tears.
I trace the hollow wind with trembling fingertips,
Seeking solace in the remnants of reflection.
But even the breeze recoils,
carrying away the echoes of doubt.
Still, in the heart of absence, a promise lingers.
A trembling pulse beneath the fractured ground.
For even the parched earth remembers the taste of water,
And I, too, recall the sweetness of surrender.

6. Reunited By The Ocean

Beneath a sky of silver light,
Two hearts rekindle in the night.
The waves, they whisper soft and low,
Of love once lost, now set aglow.
She stands where moonlight meets the sand,
He reaches out, a trembling hand.
No words are needed, eyes reveal
The longing neither could conceal.
The stars above, like diamonds bright,
Reflect their dreams, their hearts' delight.
The tide that pulled them once apart
Now sings the song of a mended heart.
The ocean hums a melody,
A tune of love, wild and free.
They dance where water greets the land,
Fingers entwined, hand in hand.
No force of time, no miles wide,
Could break the bond they hold inside.
For love, like waves, returns once more,
To find its way back to the shore.

7. My Little Mischief-Maker

There's a little boy I know so well,
With twinkling eyes and tales to tell.
He's naughty and sweet, a whirlwind of fun,
From morning's light till day is done.

He's smart and kind, both wise and bold,
With a heart of gold and laughter untold.
His giggles dance like a melody bright,
Turning my days into pure delight.

Yet when we play, he bends the rules,
Changing Ludo, his own set of rules!
"No, no! This is how it's done!"
He grins and cheats, but oh, what fun!

Sleep, you ask? Oh, what a dream!
For he bursts in with an endless stream
"Wake up! Let's play! No time to rest!"
He never tires, but I try my best.

With toys and games, he won't let me be!
Yet through the chaos, through all the noise,
I wouldn't trade him for a thousand toys.

For in his eyes, I see the truth,
A love so pure, so bright, so smooth.
And though he drives me up the wall,
I love him most, no doubt at all!

8. Between the Curtain and the Soul

Backstage she stands, a breath in time,
 The world outside begins to climb.
 The air is thick with whispered sound,
 The scent of jasmine all around.
 A fleeting moment, nerves entwine,
 The silence hums, her heart aligns.
Her fingers tremble, soft and slight,
 As she adjusts her shawl, so tight.
 The coolness of the fabric's grace,
 A comfort in this hurried place.
 Her feet, encased in silver rings,
 Can feel the stage as tension stings.
The distant notes of music swell,
 Her ears alive to every spell,
 The tabla's beat, the veena's song,
 Her mind rehearses all night long.
 A melody that stirs her soul,
 Yet nerves, like shadows, take their toll.
Her eyes are wide, her lashes wet,
 The scent of oil, her skin's duet
 With powder, incense, and the air
 A ritual she cannot spare.
 Her lips taste salt, a fleeting fear,

A breath of doubt she'll soon clear.
The lights, they call, the rhythm near,
The pulse of the earth, both sharp and clear.
She can almost see the stage ahead,
But here, behind, where nerves have led,
She stands between the past and now,
A dancer's dream, a sacred vow.
A final step, a deep inhale,
The curtain's lift, the story's tale.
The smell of sweat, the taste of time,
The touch of earth, her spirit climbs.
The music lifts her, calm, at last,
She dances now, the world surpassed.
And though the crowd will cheer her name,
She'll carry this moment just the same
The scent, the sound, the trembling feel,
The joy, the nerves, the dance's zeal.
For in her soul, both past and now,
She is the dance, she takes a bow.

9. The Ordinary Me

Average! Average! Average!
I'm just an average, simple soul,
 No special gift, no shining goal.
 I try my best, but I don't stand out,
 In a world of stars, I feel some doubt.
My grades are fine, but not the best,
 I do my work, but never rest.
 I'm just one of many in the crowd,
 My voice is soft, my head not loud.
No talents shine in my small hands,
 No grand design or future plans.
 I stumble through, not first, not last,
 A fleeting shadow from the past.
But in my heart, a truth does stay,
 That being me is okay.
 I may not lead, but I will strive,
 In my own way, I feel alive.
For even those who seem quite plain,
 Can find their joy in simple gain.
 Though I'm not gifted, I'm still enough,
 For life is sweet, and I am tough.
So here I stand, just as I am,
 An average child, a quiet span.
 And though I may not shine or boast,

I'm proud of who I am the most.

14

10. Revenge

A fire stirs within the chest,
A whispered urge, a heart's unrest.
The wounds that fester, deep and wide,
Yearn for a reckoning, none can hide.
With every breath, the shadows grow,
The urge to strike, the thirst to show.
The hurt, the loss, it fuels the flame,
And vengeance calls, no mercy, no shame.
The mind concocts, the plans unfold,
A reckoning, both fierce and cold.
In silence, scheming, heart does race,
To meet the moment, face to face.
But as the blow is struck, so fast,
A hollow victory comes at last.
For in revenge, one's soul is torn,
The price of pain, forever worn.
A bitter truth, the cost is clear,
The wound is healed, but not the fear.
Revenge, though sweet, leaves scars so deep,
A promise made, a promise to keep.

11. Silent Screams

In shadows deep, where silence lies,
  A heart beats loud, but no one tries.
  The lips are sealed, the breath held tight,
  A scream is born in endless night.
The world goes on, a steady flow,
  But within, the storm begins to grow.
  The eyes are wide, yet no one sees,
  The quiet plea, the whispered plea.
A scream, so loud, it shakes the soul,
  Yet trapped inside, it takes its toll.
  The throat is choked, the voice is mute,
  A battle fought, but none to loot.
The hands, they tremble, weak and raw,
  But still, no sound, no painful awe.
  It claws the mind, it rips apart,
  A silent scream within the heart.
It echoes far, but none can hear,
  A cry for help, a drowning fear.
  A scream for freedom, lost in space,
  In silent chains, she holds her place.
And yet, with time, the voice will rise,
  Not in a shout, but in quiet skies
  A silent scream, now fierce and true,
  The world may hear, but none will view.

12. A Beautiful Decay

In the wrinkles etched like rivers deep,
  Where time has walked and memories sleep,
  There lies a beauty, soft and slow,
  In every line, in every glow.
The silver strands that crown the brow,
  Are not of loss, but wisdom's vow,
  A tale of days well spent and true,
  Each whispering a shade of you.
The hands that tremble, worn with grace,
  Hold stories in their gentle trace,
  Of love, of laughter, of tears once shed,
  Now woven in the life you've led.
In the softening dusk of fading sight,
  The soul shines clearer, burning bright.
  For beauty, though it wears away,
  Is not the youth, but the love we say.
In every step, in every sigh,
  In the quiet where the echoes lie,
  There blooms a beauty, soft and free
  The art of growing old, you see.
For in decay, there's life anew,
  A gentle grace, a richer hue,
  A beauty that the years will keep
  A beautiful decay, so deep.

13. A Father's love, A Daughter's Heart

A father's arms, a safe embrace,
 A daughter's smile, a shining grace.
 He watches her with tender eyes,
 As time, like a river, swiftly flies.
From tiny hands that reach for his,
 To giggles shared in quiet bliss.
 He guides her steps, both soft and true,
 With every lesson, love shines through.
Her laughter echoes in his heart,
 A bond that'll never drift apart.
 Through every tear, through every cheer,
 He's always there, forever near.
A daughter grows, her world expands,
 Yet in his heart, she still holds his hand.
 No matter where life takes her far,
 She'll always be his shining star.
In moments small and moments grand,
 A father and daughter hand in hand,
 A love so pure, so sweet, so bright,
 That fills the world with warmth and light.

14. Guru-Shishya Parampara

In silence deep, the lessons flow,
A sacred bond, where wisdom grows.
The Guru's light, so pure, so bright,
Guides the soul through darkest night.
With gentle words, with knowing eyes,
The Guru lifts, the spirit flies.
The Shishya seeks, with heart sincere,
To learn, to grow, to persevere.
Through ages past, this path remains,
A lineage strong that ever sustains.
From teacher's soul to student's heart,
The sacred flame shall never part.
The Guru's grace, the Shishya's quest,
Together they strive, to be their best.
A dance of knowledge, trust, and care,
A bond divine, beyond compare.
In the silence of each lesson's grace,
The Guru's truth, the Shishya's face,
Reflects the light that forever burns,
In the eternal cycle that always turns.
Through this Parampara, we find our way,
In each moment, each word they say,

For the Guru's love, and the Shishya's will,
Are the forces that guide us still.

15. Lost in the Echoes of Time

Lost in the echoes of time I roam,
 Wandering through ages, far from home.
 Whispers of moments, fading and deep,
 Echoes of memories, secrets they keep.
The clock ticks softly, yet loud in my mind,
 Leaving behind what it's destined to find.
 A world of shadows, once bright and alive,
 Now distant, in silence, they strive to survive.
In the dance of the stars, I trace the unknown,
 A traveler of time, but never alone.
 Each echo a heartbeat, a story once told,
 Now drifting like dust, in the winds of the cold.
Through centuries passed, I walk on the thread,
 Chasing the voices of those long dead.
 In the vastness of time, I've lost track of when,
 Yet I search for the echoes again and again.
For though time may fade and memories may die,
 In the echoes, I'll always be able to fly.
 Lost in the echoes of time, I remain,
 Bound by its whispers, its joy and its pain.

16. Seasons of Her Soul

She came like dawn with laughter bright,
Wrapped in her parents' arms so tight,
A world of lullabies and skies,
Of bedtime tales and sleepy eyes.
They taught her how to walk and dream,
To chase the stars, to swim upstream,
Her mother's kiss, her father's smile,
Her world, for them, was worth the while.
Then came the days of whispered names,
Of scribbled hearts and hallway games,
A boy who saw her just that way,
First love, so warm and new and fey.
She stumbled, soared, she learned the ache,
Of promises that youth can break,
But in the shards, she found a grace,
A mirror's truth, her own embrace.
She bloomed in time, in full control,
With self-love dancing in her soul.
And love came not as storms or fire,
But steady hands and shared desire.
She found her home in vows once said,
In laughter shared and tears once shed,
A husband's warmth, the evening tea,
The gentle hum of "you and me."

Then tiny feet and messy days,
 The chaos shaped in sweetest ways,
 She loved again, in brand-new hues,
 In crayon scribbles, untied shoes.
Her children grew, the seasons spun,
 A thousand moons, a thousand suns,
 Her house grew still, yet full of sound,
 Of echoes time had wrapped around.
Now silver lines her flowing hair,
 She sits beside a twilight air,
 Recalling days like autumn leaves,
 The way love came and softly weaved.
From parents' arms to lovers' touch,
 To holding hands that meant so much,
 To finding self through joy and strife,
 She'd lived a thousand lives in life.
And as her breath begins to slow,
 The wind recalls what she did know,
 That love, in all its quiet grace,
 Had been her life's most sacred place.
She smiles and sighs, the end so near,
 While all her yesterdays draw near,
 And in the hush, a final breath,
 She finds her peace in love and death.

17. The Ocean's Lullaby

The moon hangs low in a velvet sky,
A silver eye that dreams on high.
Its beams like fingers soft and slow
Caress the waves in rhythmic flow.
The sea, in shimmered silence, sighs,
Reflecting light in lullabies.
Each crest a kiss, each trough a prayer,
As moonlight dances everywhere.
A path of pearl on waters wide
Invites the stars to slip and glide.
They twinkle, hush, and drift in tune
With secrets only known to moon.
No voices stir, no winds arise,
Just ocean breath and starlit skies.
The night is deep, yet full of grace,
Where moonlight finds the sea's embrace.

18. Where Dreams Begin

The wind it speaks in silver sighs,
 Through trees that dance beneath the skies.
 It tells of places far and wide,
 Of oceans deep and mountains' pride.
A leaf may fall, a petal spin,
 A tale begins where dreams begin.
 Soft footprints vanish in the sand,
 Yet echoes stay, like hearts unplanned.
So let the wind pass through your soul,
 A breath of truth, a voice made whole.
 It calls you not to simply stay,
 But find your wings and fly away.

19. The Quite Beneath

Beneath the noise, beneath the name,
Beyond the masks we learn to claim,
There lies a stillness, dark and wide,
A place the world forgets to find.
No mirror speaks the truth you seek,
No praise can hush the soul's mystique.
For in the cracks, the quiet seams,
We stitch ourselves from shattered dreams.
We are not stars, but burning flame,
Not bound by past, nor carved by shame.
The path is not a line, but bend,
Where endings meet, and then transcend.
So dig, unearth the buried thread,
The part of you not born, but bred
In silence, ache, and sacred strife,
The hidden forge that makes a life.

20. What The Ashes Say

The fire burned, and left no sound,
 Just hollow air and blackened ground.
  Where laughter lived and love once lay,
  Now silence grows in shades of gray.
But ashes speak in secret ways,
 Of every night and all its days,
 They whisper not of all that's gone,
 But of the strength to still go on.
You hold the pain like folded wings,
 A bird that's learned what sorrow sings.
 Yet still, it stirs, your breath, your chest,
 A restless hope that will not rest.
For healing isn't clean or bright,
 It crawls through shadow, learns the night.
 And when it speaks, it doesn't cry,
 It simply says: *you did not die*

21. The Name I Never Spoke

I've worn a thousand faces well,
 Each one a story I could sell.
 But in the mirror, late and low,
 There's someone I still do not know.
They call me kind, they call me strong,
 A thousand names, and all feel wrong.
 For none have touched the quiet thread
 That ties my soul to what's unsaid.
I walk the world, both guest and ghost,
 Not quite at home, not fully lost.
 The sky is mine, but not the ground,
 I speak in echoes, not in sound.
Yet somewhere deep, beneath the skin,
 A softer voice begins to spin,
 Not loud, not sure, but bold and true:
 A name that's mine, not made for you.

www.ingramcontent.com/pod-product-compliance
Lightning Source LLC
La Vergne TN
LVHW010954200726
843509LV00013B/2417